P9-DEP-939

SCHOLASTIC INC.
New York Toronto London Auckland Sydney
Mexico City New Delhi Hong Kong

Dedicated to all of our families

We like to feel secure and safe.
Somedays, the rut is the best place to be.

All rights reserved. No part of this publication may be reproduced, or stored in a retrieval system, or transmitted in any form or by any means, electronic, mechanical, photocopying, recording, or otherwise, without written permission of the publisher. For information regarding permission, write to Scholastic, Inc., Attention: Permission Department, 557 Broadway, New York, NY 10012.

Copyright © 2002 by Scholastic Inc
Scholastic and associated logos are trademarks and/or registered trademarks of Scholastic Inc
ISBN 0-439-44246-X

12 11 10 9 8 7 6 5 4 3 2 1 00 01 02 03 04

Book Design by Bill Henderson
Printed and bound in the U.S.A.

First Printing, July 2002

Meet the Authors

First Grade Class, H. Byron Masterson Elementary School, Kennett, MO

Standing, left to right: Rebecca Smith, Jay Edgington, Kayla McBay, Jamie Ellington, Cameron Harper, William Thomas, Anna Kay Hilburn, Amy Johnson, Keisha Walker, Brian Stracener

Sitting, left to right: Chandler Agee, Jordan Garza, Josh Harmon, Jordan Tefft, Bryce McPherson, Monique Gray, Onterria Carter, Shawn Birmingham

On September 11, 2001, many bad things happened.

September 12th
was a new day.
We knew
everything
would be all
right.

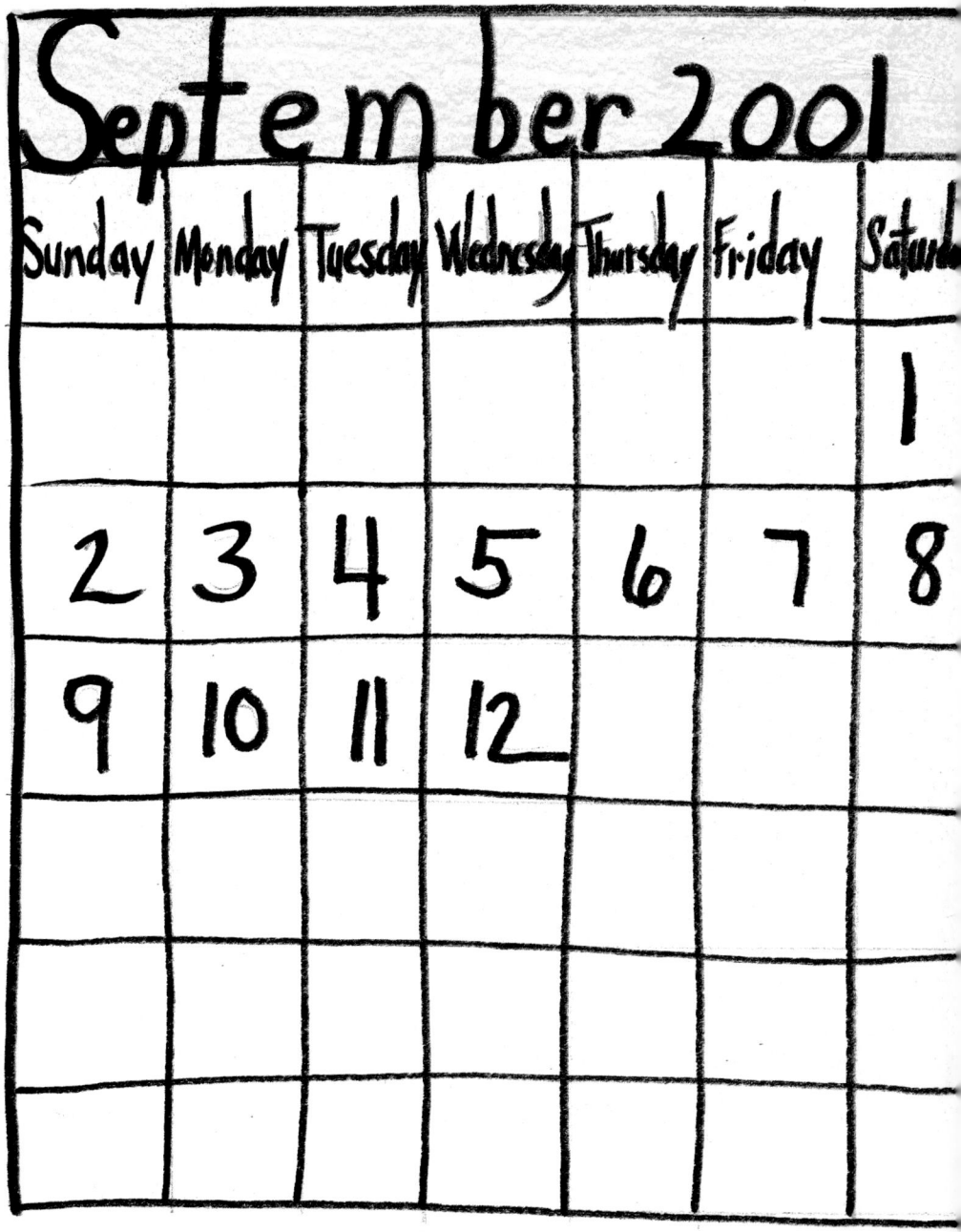

because...

the sun came up and

the birds started
to sing again.

We came
to school
the same
way.

We knew everything would be all right when we saw our teacher smiling at the door.

We said the pledge like always.

We sang the National Anthem very loudly.

V.I.P dining area

Aa Bb Cc Dd Ee Ff Gg Hh Ii Jj Kk Ll Mm
Xx Y
Our teacher sat and read
us lots of good books.
Mrs.
Robertson

We had recess again.

We knew everything would be all right because we had homework.

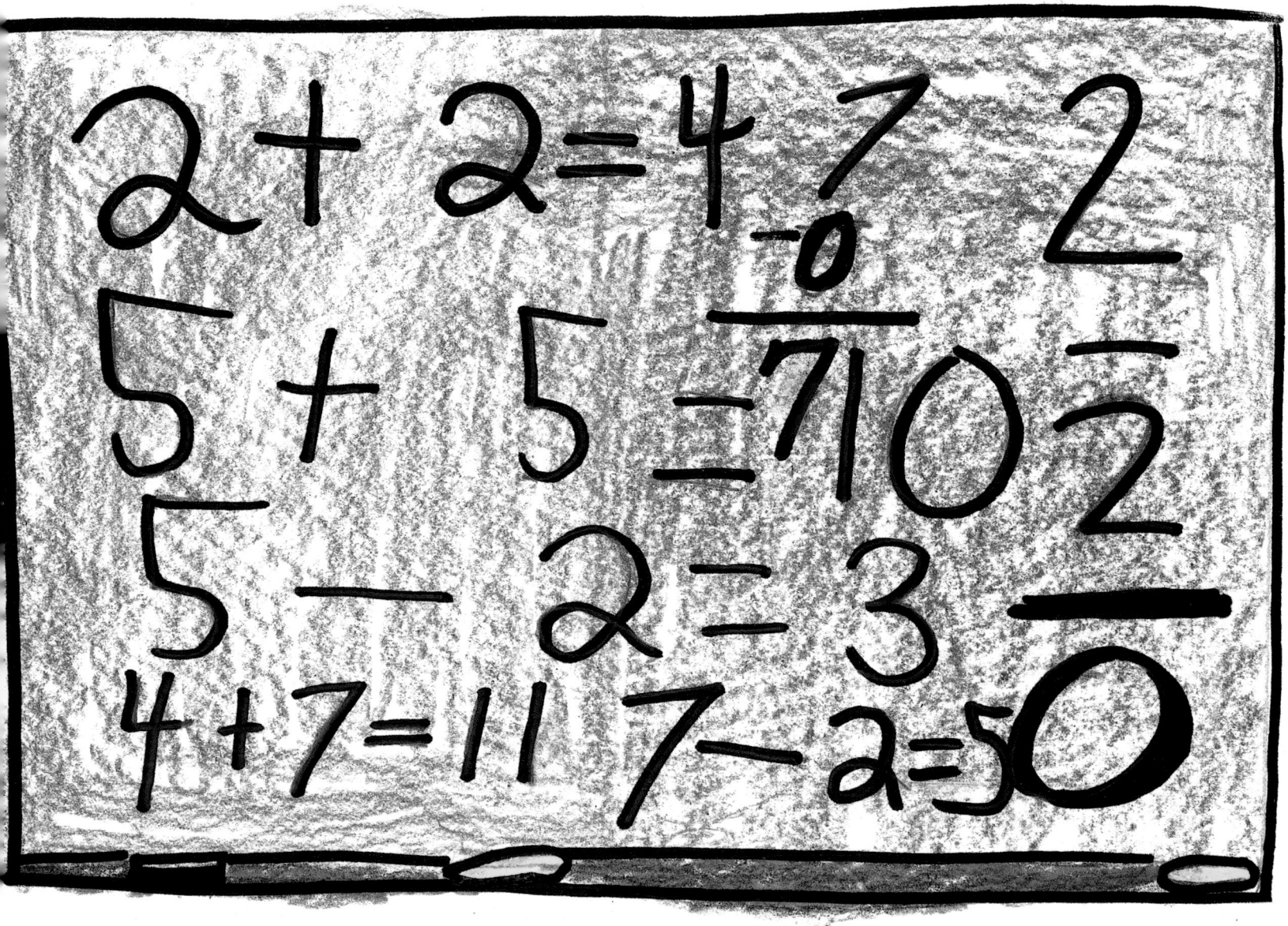

2+2 still added up to 4.

Our thought for the day became "America United."

We saw
lots of flags.

Red, white and blue suddenly became everyone's favorite colors.

On television we heard our President tell us everything would be all right.

On September 12th, our parents
still tucked us in our warm, safe beds.

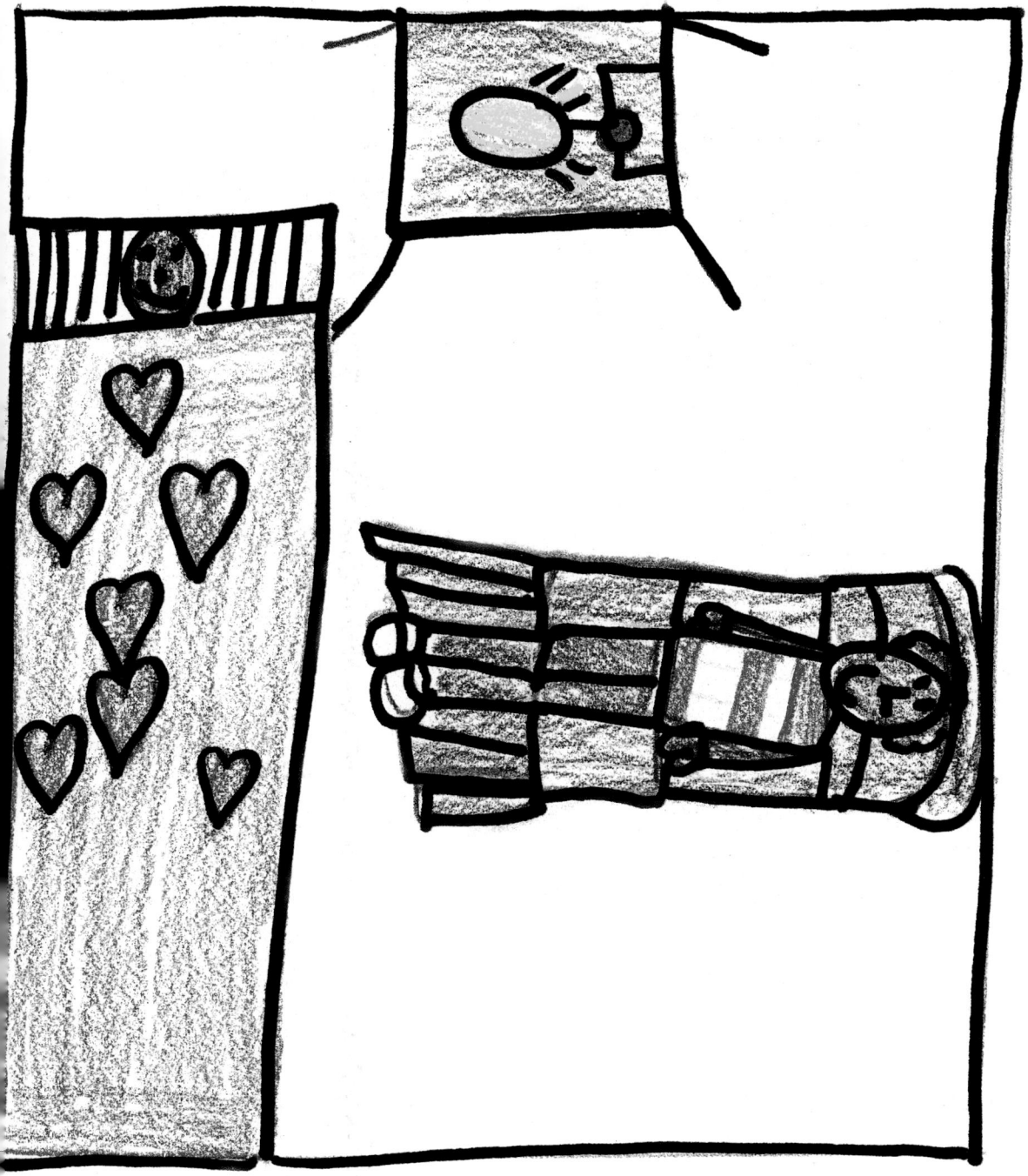

Our parents talked to us about the bad things that had happened the day before.

We knew we would be all right
because our parents said they loved us.

We knew everything would be all right because the stars and moon came out and America went to sleep.

And the next morning
the sun came up again.

NOT
The End.